Thoughts, Just Thoughts

A collection of a lifetime of thoughts.

By Michael Carter

Dedication

This book is dedicated to the memory of my wife, Josefina (Chepa) Gonzales y Mendoza, who passed away from ovarian cancer on August 1, 2021, at 9:06 PM.

Always in my thoughts, forever in my heart.

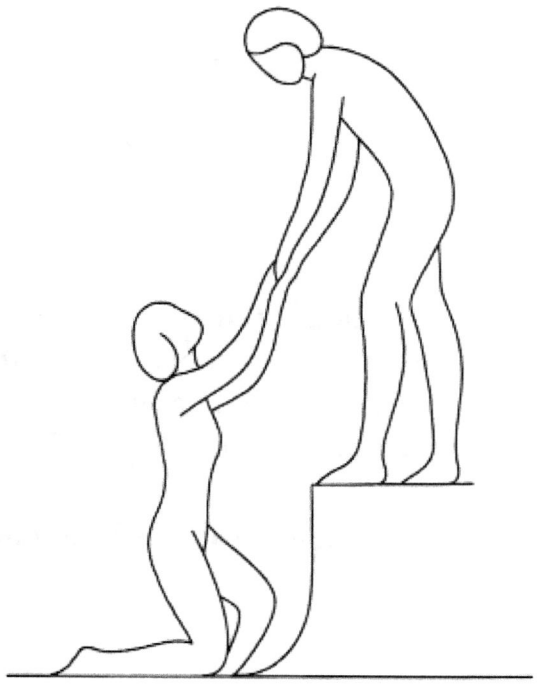

Never look down on someone unless you are helping them up.

◆▸◆◂◆

Is time an invention or discovery of man?

◆▸◆◂◆

There are no atheists in a foxhole.

◆▸◆◂◆

There is only one human race.
We are all sisters and brothers.

◆▸◆◂◆

Where does the white go when the snow melts?

◆▸◆◂◆

Coincidence is God's way of remaining anonymous.
Albert Einstein

If you can dream it, you can do it.
Walt Disney

The pen is mightier than the sword.
Edward Bulwer-Lytton

To live your life in your way,
to reach for the goals you have set for yourself,
to be the person you want to be.
That is success.

The day the soldiers stop bringing you their problems is the day you stopped leading them. They have either lost confidence that you can help them or concluded that you do not care. Either case is a failure in leadership.
Colin Powell

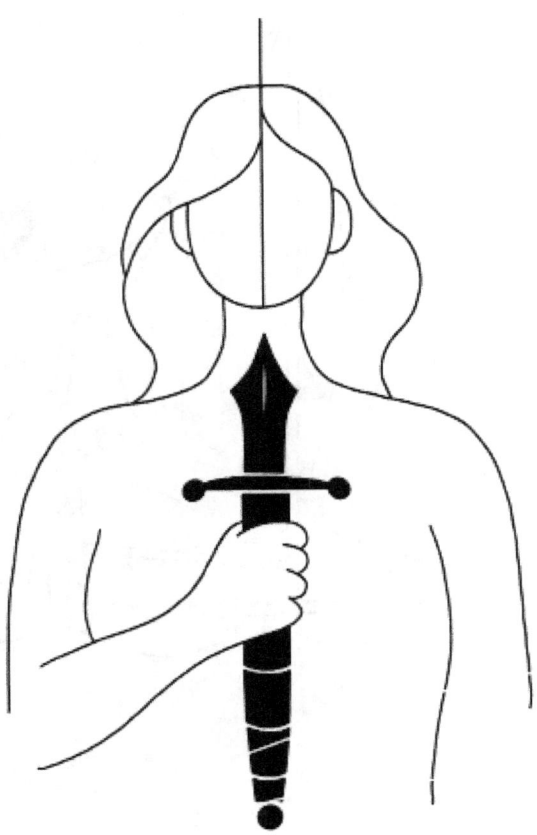

Are we born with memories of our past lives?

Hate is heavy; love is light.
Judge Esther Salas

As we make the journey through life, we can't direct the wind, but we can adjust our sails.

You can do anything for 20 minutes except hold your breath.
Rosalyn Carter

The door to love is never closed.

If God has to make but one decision in all of eternity, the future not only exists but is unpredictable.

If a man does not keep pace with his companions,
perhaps it is because he hears a different drummer.

Let him step to the music which he hears,
however measured or far away.
Henry David Thoreau

The supreme happiness of life is the conviction of being
loved for yourself, or more correctly,
being loved in spite of yourself.
Victor Hugo

Life is filled with opportunities and challenges.

Change is the only constant in life.

Nothing matters more than more years together.

The best way to predict the future is to be part of it.

⬤▸◉◂⬤

You're never too old to do what needs to be done.

⬤▸◉◂⬤

A complete definition of a successful marriage can be found in almost any book on elementary psychology. Indeed, entire books have been written on this notable and inveterate institution into which so many of us have ventured. Because a working definition is elusive, I feel it can best be defined and explained by the analogy formed between a successful marriage and a river.

A river starts its journey by gathering and acquiring many tributaries at its headwaters. In a successful marriage, these tributaries are the gathering and acquiring of love, compassion, understanding, and agreement. As the river's journey continues, it experiences many experiences, many situations, both good and bad, that it must cope with successfully. For instance, it will encounter rapids, and unless the river maintains control, the results to the surroundings will be disastrous. In its life, a river may contend with a waterfall. These falls, too, could be disastrous because of the trauma and the eroding of the river's bed.

⬤▸◉◂⬤

But rivers always recover from these falls; some marriages do not. Those that do recover will continue to find deep pools of contentment and peace of mind. The river and a successful marriage may wind back and forth, but it will never lose its sense of direction toward its ultimate destination. But here, the analogy ends, for a river will eventually become lost in the immensity of an ocean.

A successful marriage has no end—unless it had no beginning. And then it too will dry up and be no more.

⚬⚬⚬

Build bridges, not walls.

⚬⚬⚬

Try not to judge another person even if you have walked a mile in their shoes.

Michael Carter

Michael Carter

Life is a song; love is the music.

◆►◆◄◆

It doesn't matter where we go in life,
it's who you have beside you along the way.

◆►◆◄◆

To live your life in your way,
to reach for the goals you have set for yourself,
to be the person you want to be.
That is success.

◆►◆◄◆

No one can make you feel inferior without your permission.
Eleanor Roosevelt

◆►◆◄◆

All men have their frailties,
And whoever looks for a friend without imperfections
Will never find what he seeks.

We love ourselves notwithstanding our faults,
and we ought to love our friends in like manner.
Cyrus the Great

━►•◄━

What we receive from any relationship
depends not just on what we want to give,
but also on what we want to receive.

━►•◄━

I've learned that people will forget what you said, people will
forget what you did,
but people will never forget how you made them feel.
Maya Angelou

━►•◄━

You may not have control over what happens to you,
but you do have control over how you respond.

━►•◄━

Gettin' old ain't for wimps.

━►•◄━

We're all part of the tree of evolution; we all share common roots.

Michael Carter

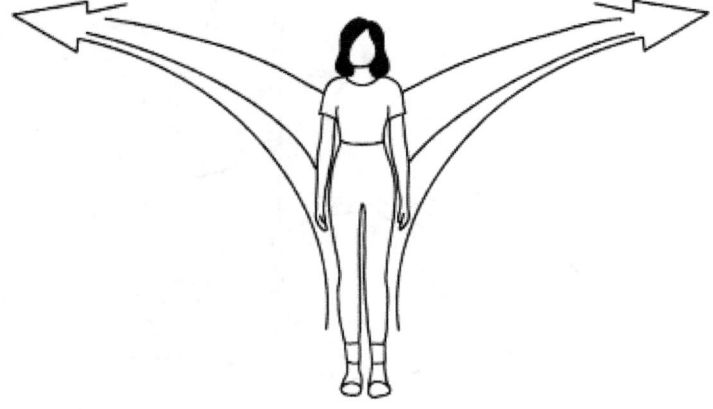

Do all living organisms: humans, animals, plants, and insects, have a soul and spirit? If so, where did the soul and spirit come from, and where do they go when the organism dies?

A bad attitude is like a flat tire;
You can't go anywhere until you change it.

No relationship is without problems and challenges,
not if it has any depth.

Twenty years from now you will be more disappointed by the things you didn't do than by the ones you did do.

So, throw off the bowlines. Sail away from the safe harbor.
Catch the trade winds in your sails.
Explore. Dream. Discover.
Mark Twain

"Hey Dad, you gotta minute."
Yeh, Dad, you had a minute. You had a lot of minutes.

◆▸◈◂◆

Remember the time I lost my new softball in the blackberry bush? I knew you were already late for work, but you saw that big tear just starting to roll down my cheek, and you put your hand on my shoulder and said, "Come on, son, we'll find it." Dad, you always had time to play another game of catch, get my kite out of the tree, or just sit and be my friend. "Hey, Dad, I need your help." Six years old, and I'd forgotten how to tie my shoes. Remember that? It seems a long time ago when I'd sit on your lap and ask you to read me just one more story. And then I'd fall asleep. I don't remember saying "Thanks Dad," at least not enough. Lotta years since then. One day, I didn't think I wanted to be your little boy anymore; I thought I was too big for that. You know, we don't get a chance to talk much these days, and I guess I've been holding a few things back.

"Listen up, Dad, 'cause your little boy has something to say."

"Hey Dad, I love you."
Call home tonight.
Someone wants to listen.

◆▸◈◂◆

19

Michael Carter

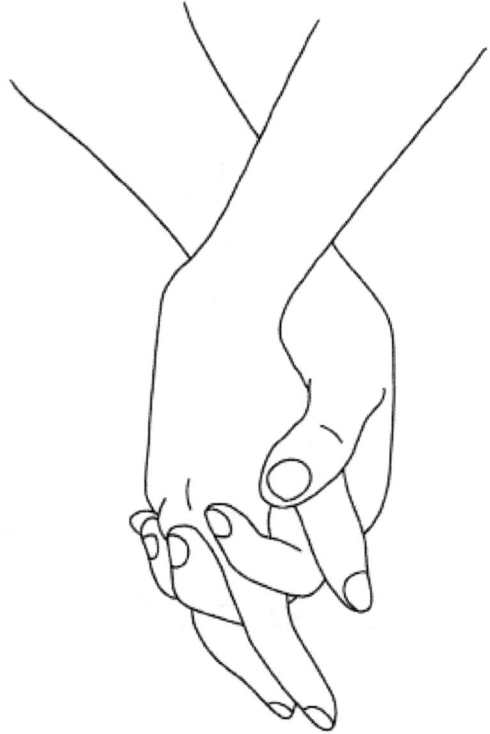

The following was written by me for my son and fiancée and read at their wedding.

Love is . . .

Love is caring, caring that the other person is happy with themselves and what's going on. Caring enough to be as close as needed. Caring that the harmony is always heard.

Love is understanding what's important to the other person. Understanding when they need help and when they don't.

Love is moving out of the way when the person needs space and knowing that sometimes we all need to be alone.

Love is the trust that your feelings will always be handled with dignity and respect. The trust of knowing the other person will never do anything to intentionally hurt you.

Love is wanting to save the last dance.

Love is fun.

Love is laughing, and love is crying when nothing else works.

Love is a night on the town at McDonald's.

Love is never being alone.

Love is wanting to call each day when you're away, and love is wanting to go home.

Love is never underestimating the other person nor taking them for granted.

Love is doing your own thing together.

Love is not taking the last scoop of ice cream.

Love is the absence of all fear, as truth is the absence of all guilt.

Love is giving a gift for the best reason of all – because you just want to.

Love is a special gift. A special feeling that makes everything else happen and that brings two people together in a special way.

Love is limitless.

⬥⟩⬥⟨⬥

Maybe the purpose of our life is to gain a better understanding and reason of our soul and spirit and who, or what established our purpose.

⬥⟩⬥⟨⬥

The smallest deed is better than the grandest intention.

⬥⟩⬥⟨⬥

We're all part of the tree of evolution; we all share common roots.

⬥

We can't be angry and sensible at the same time.

⬥

Can Artificial Intelligence (AI) help cure ovarian cancer?

⬥

Children are not born with hatred. They learn this from their parents, relatives, siblings, and friends and from their political environment.

⬥

All the flowers of all the tomorrows are in the seeds of today.
Chinese Proverb

⬥

Creativity in business has constraints – usually done to solve a problem. Whereas an artist is completely free to express an idea with no restrictions.

⬥

Michael Carter

All of us occasionally dwell on the past, sometimes negative. Creativity dwells on a positive future and concentrates on what is yet to be.

———

Both politicians and diapers need to be changed often and for the same reasons.

———

Life is like a camera.
Just focus on what's important.
Capture the good times.
Develop from the negatives and if things don't turn out,
take another shot.
Mark Twain

———

Two battles exist in each of us.
Evil and anger, and love and hope.
Which one wins?
The one you feed.

———

Can the concept of absoluteness co-exist with the concept of time?
Is there a master plan? If so, by whom?
The answer is in the question.

———

The only things we can physically experience are those that we experience through one or more of our five senses. Everything else is either a thought based on anticipation or a memory.

———

You know you've reached old age when you think you still know how, pretty sure you still can, but you can't remember the last time you did.

———

Success is a decision.

———

31

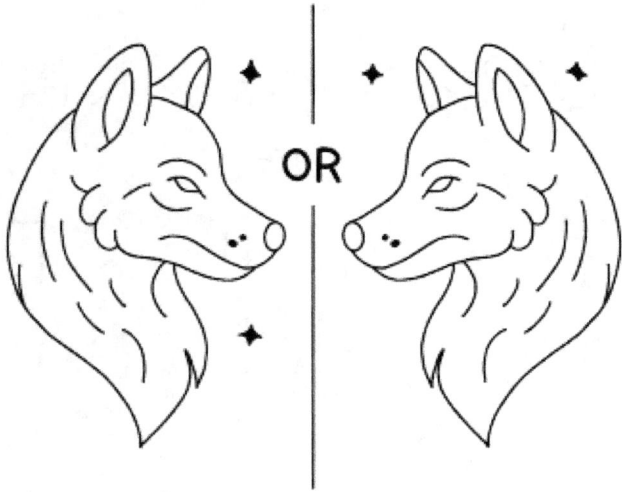

OR

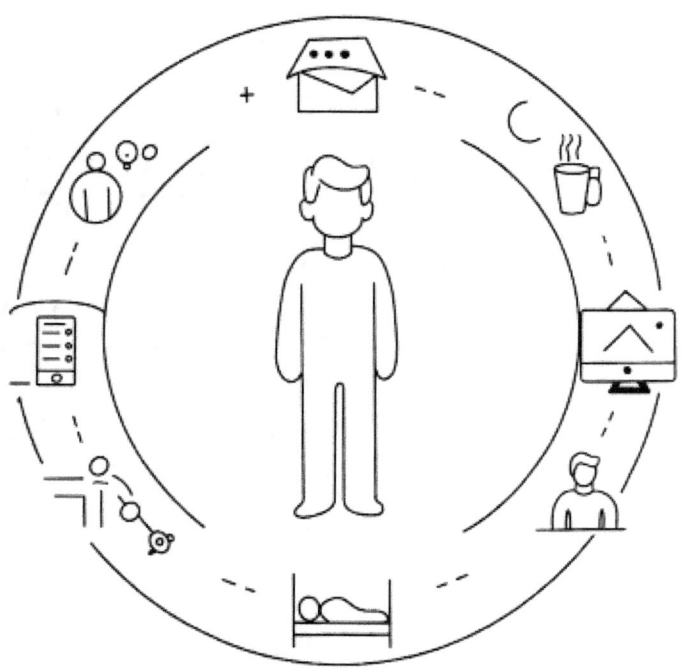

A man is a success if he gets up in the morning, goes to bed at night
and in between does what he wants to do.
Bob Dylan

The world is moving so fast these days that the man who says it
can't be done is generally interrupted by the man who is doing it.
Elbert Hubbard

The shell must break before the bird can fly.
Alfred Tennyson

Patience is also a form of action.
Auguste Rodin

When you give the kind of love that expects nothing in return,
you are never disappointed.

There is no elevator to success; you have to take the stairs.
Zig Ziglar

The reasonable man adapts himself to the world. The unreasonable
man persists in trying to adapt the world to himself. Therefore, all
progress depends on the unreasonable man.
G.B. Shaw

I won't try to twist your arm – won't twist your head either.

I do my thing and you do your thing.
I am not in this world to live up to your expectations
And you are not in this world to live up to mine.
You are you, and I am I
And if by chance we find each other
it's beautiful.
Fritz Perls

Michael Carter

A friend is a present you give yourself.
Robert Louis Stevenson

━►•◄━

No man is rich enough to buy back his past.
Oscar Wilde

━►•◄━

Love
Love is patient, love is kind, and is not jealous;
love does not brag and is not arrogant,
does not act unbecomingly;
it does not seek its own, is not provoked,
does not take into account a wrong suffered,
does not rejoice in unrighteousness,
but rejoices with the truth; bears all things,
believes all things, hopes all things, endures all things.
Love never fails.
1 Corinthians 13: 4-8

━►•◄━

I shall pass through this world but once.
Any good thing, therefore, that I can do or any kindness
I can show to any fellow human being; let me do it now.
Let me not defer nor neglect it;
for I shall not pass this way again.
Stephen Grellet

Limits, like fears, are often just an illusion.
Michael Jordan

It's not how you start but how you finish.
Michael Phelps

An old Arabian proverb tells of four things that never return:
the spoken word,
the spent arrow,
the past life,
and the unused opportunity.

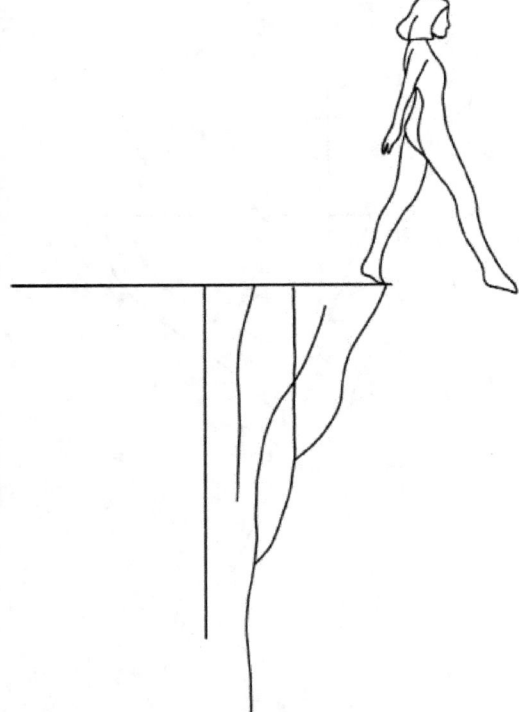

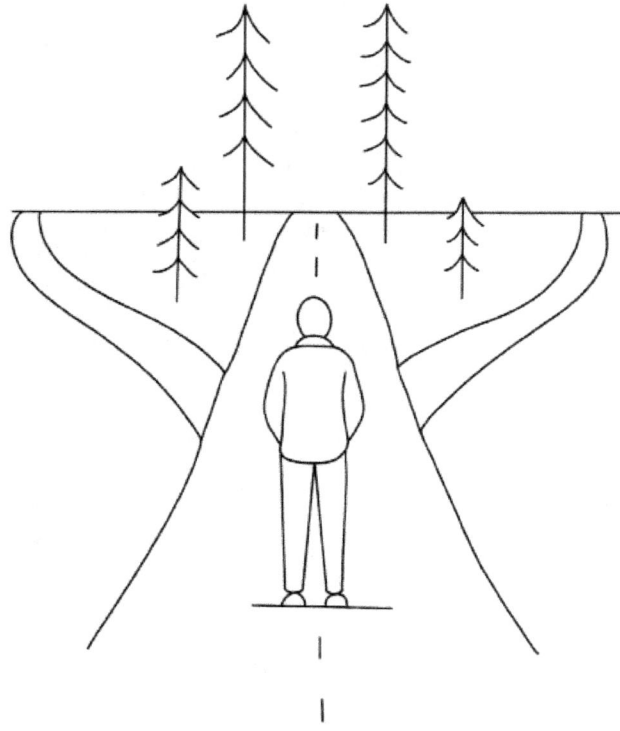

Challenges are what makes life interesting and overcoming them
is what makes life meaningful.
Joshua Marine

⬤⬤⬤

Sometimes you have to take a step back to move forward.
Erika Taylor

⬤⬤⬤

Start where you are, use what you have, do what you can.
Arthur Ashe

⬤⬤⬤

For as long as we are friends, I must express my feelings,
and hope – no pray – that my expression will be gentle enough for
you to easily manage.

⬤⬤⬤

I shall be telling this with a sigh somewhere ages and ages hence;
two roads diverged in a wood, and I, I took the one less traveled
and that has made all the difference.
Robert Frost

Trust is like yesterday.
Once it's gone, it can never return.

◆▸●◂◆

The only words better than I do are the words: I always will.
Rod Sadleir

◆▸●◂◆

Minds are like parachutes; they only function when they are open.
Thomas Dewar

◆▸●◂◆

Believe you can and you're halfway there.
Theodore Roosevelt

◆▸●◂◆

Life is like riding a bicycle. To keep your balance,
you must keep on moving.
Albert Einstein

◆▸●◂◆

Each day, you find a way into my thoughts.

Be the change you wish to see in the world.
Gandhi

Be the reason someone smiles today.

A cloudy day is no match for a sunny disposition.

We can't go back and change the beginning, but we can begin where we are and change the ending.

One day, you will thank yourself for never giving up.
Rod Sadleir

The handshake is mightier than the sword.

The closer your smile, the closer you are to my heart.

Do animals laugh?

My *I Do* Vows

I do promise to love you completely and forever – always.
I do remember the first time we met.
I do believe we were met for each other.
I do thank you for being the person you are.
I do want you to know how much your love means to me.
I do think of the warmth you give me with you in my heart.
I do think of the future with you, and I know my life will be complete.
I do not wonder what life would be like without you,
I don't go there.

Don't walk in front of me
I may not follow.
Don't walk behind me
I may not lead.
Walk beside me
and just be my friend.
Camus

What I gave, I have.
What I spent, I had.
What I kept, I lost.
An old Epitaph

———

Always leave room in your affections
to bury the faults of your friends.

———

Every man should have a fair-sized cemetery
in which to bury the faults of his friends.
Henry Ward Beecher

———

The cause of the argument is much
less important than the solution.

———

To preserve a friend, three things are necessary:
to honor him present,
to praise him absent,
and assist him in his necessities.
From the Italian

———

Who seeks a friend without a fault remains without one.
Proverb from the Turkish

———

The wider your appeal, the more shallow it is.
Stendahl

———

All of men's miseries derive from
not being able to sit at a table in a room alone.
Blasé Pascal

———

Michael Carter

The clouds which appear darkest in the distance
are the ones that the wind blows the other way.
Indian Proverb

❖

There is only one thing in the world worse than being talked
about, and that is not being talked about.
Oscar Wilde

❖

Because our relationship is based on honesty and fairness,
There is no need to test each other.

❖

It is wonderful to find someone whom I don't need to play games
with and who lives up to everything I consider
important, right, and beautiful.
Susan Polis Schultz

❖

The more a man knows, the more he forgives.
Anonymous

Character is the ability to carry through
a resolution after the mood has left you.

—>•<—

Every mountain has at least two valleys.
Anonymous

—>•<—

Children need models more than they need critics.
Joseph Joubert

—>•<—

The only conquests which are permanent,
and leave no regrets,
are our conquests over ourselves.
Napoleon

—>•<—

Time ripens all things. No man is born wise.
Cervantes

—>•<—

No man is free who is not master of himself.
Epictetus

Michael Carter

Time is infinitely long and each day is a vessel into which a great
deal may be poured, if one will actually fill it up.
Johann Wolfgang von Goethe

With every mistake, we walk down the road of learning and hope.

Time itself flows on with constant motion, just like a river;
for no more than a river can the fleeting hour standstill.

What was before is left behind, that which was not comes to be,
and every minute gives place to another.
Ovid

Life is too short to wake up in the morning with regrets.
So, love the people who treat you right,
forgive the ones who don't and believe that everything happens
for a reason.

＊＊＊

If you get the chance, take it.
If it changes your life, let it.
Nobody said it would be easy.
They just promised it would be worth it.
Dr. Seuss

＊＊＊

Let nothing dim the light that shines within.
Maya Angelou

＊＊＊

Success is liking yourself, liking what you do,
and liking how you do it.
Maya Angelou

＊＊＊

Soul mates are like puzzle pieces – a perfect fit.

Maybe you don't 'find' your soul mate but 'become' soul mates.
You evolve into a soul mate relationship.
Dr. Shauna H. Springer

Maybe we don't 'find' our soul mate but create one through years
of learning by navigating challenges, creating a family, and loving
each other through all the happy and hard times.

Soul mates challenge each of us to transcend into a higher state of
consciousness.
Suzana E. Flores

World peace through world love. It'll work both ways.

Do all the little things right, and you never have to worry about
the big things.

May there just be peace in your mind and compassion in your soul.

❂

Each and every day, when I first see the light in your eyes and your beautiful face, you are my second sunrise.

❂

We are what our thoughts have made us;
so take care about what you think.
Words are secondary.
Thoughts live; they travel far.
Swami Vivekananda

❂

For every minute you are angry, you lose sixty seconds of happiness.
Ralph Waldo Emerson

❂

There are two ways to be. One is at war with reality and the other is at peace.
Bryan Katie

❂

You're never too important to not be nice to people.
Jon Batiste

❧

The most important thing is to find out what is the most important thing.
Shunryu Suzuki

❧

We are shaped by our thoughts; we become what we think. When the mind is pure, joy follows like a shadow that never leaves.
Buddha

❧

We are addicted to our thoughts.
We cannot change anything if we cannot change our thoughts.
Santosh Kalwar

❧

In three words, I can sum up everything I have learned about life:
It goes on.
Robert Frost

❖❖❖❖

May we always need one another, not so much to fill our emptiness
as to know our fullness.

❖❖❖❖

Forever is composed of nows.
Emily Dickinson

❖❖❖❖

Forever in heaven.
Norwegian saying

❖❖❖❖

It only takes a moment to make a moment.

❖❖❖❖

Sometimes, silence is the best support we can give someone.

❖❖❖❖

We have only one tool with which to fight for democracy, and
that is democracy.

❖❖❖❖

Michael Carter

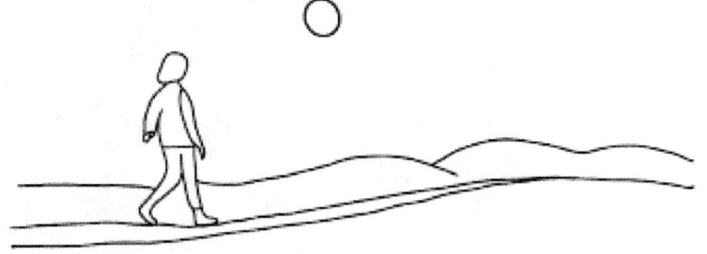

Who you think you are each day,
completely determines the universe you live in.
Ram Dass

$\rightarrow\rightarrow\bullet\leftarrow\rightarrow$

If we are facing in the right direction, all we have to do is keep
walking.
Buddhist proverb

$\rightarrow\rightarrow\bullet\leftarrow\rightarrow$

The key to everything: give yourself permission to be who you
really are.
Susan Cain

$\rightarrow\rightarrow\bullet\leftarrow\rightarrow$

We think too much and feel too little.
Charlie Chaplin

$\rightarrow\rightarrow\bullet\leftarrow\rightarrow$

Where does a thought go when it's forgotten?
Sigmund Freud

$\rightarrow\rightarrow\bullet\leftarrow\rightarrow$

He who is untrue to his own cause cannot command the respect
of others.
Albert Einstein

❖

We have never arrived.
We are in a constant state of becoming.
Bob Dylan

❖

God is a comedian playing to an audience
too afraid to laugh.
H.L. Mencken

❖

The more man meditates upon good thoughts, the better will be
his world and the world at large.
Confucius

❖

I never learned anything when I was talking.
Larry King

A clear rejection is always better than a fake promise.
Zig Ziglar

Don't push the river; let the river flow.
Arianna Huffington

Direction matters more than speed.
Shane Parrish

Those who stand for nothing fall for anything.
Alexander Hamilton

Life is like riding a bicycle. To keep your balance, you must keep moving.
Albert Einstein

◆▸●◂◆

All the flowers of all the tomorrows
are in the seeds of today.
Chinese Proverb

◆▸●◂◆

Be the change you wish to see in the world.
Gandhi

◆▸●◂◆

Be the reason someone smiles today.

◆▸●◂◆

Success is a decision.

◆▸●◂◆

To the world, you may be just one person, but to one person, you may be the world.

It is foolish to fear the inevitable.

You are as good as the best thing you've ever done.

It is a poor thing to fear that which is inevitable.

Friendship is two bodies and one mind.

Take the time and make an effort to enjoy
those things that bring you happiness in whatever time you may
have left.

I need to focus on the happiness I have, including family, friends,
and memories, and not dwell on those things that are gone and
over which I have no control.

Open the window of your heart to let in the love.

An investment in knowledge pays the best interest.
Benjamin Franklin

You can't be smart and angry at the same time.

⟐

Sometimes, the path cannot be seen.
Go where your passion leads you.

⟐

The best mirror is a good friend.

⟐

The price of greatness is responsibility.
Winston Churchill

⟐

He who dares not offend cannot be honest.
Thomas Payne

⟐

When life gets blurry, adjust your focus.

⟐

You can stand by and see what happens or stand up and make it happen.

⟐

Trees don't grow to the sky.
German Proverb

It doesn't matter where you go in life,
it's who you have beside you along the way.

❖❖❖

Life is better when we're together.

❖❖❖

Breath in – inhale love.
Breath out – exhale gratitude.

❖❖❖

Love is all you need.

❖❖❖

You will forever be my always.

❖❖❖

May love, not fear, be the engine of change.

❖❖❖

Success is the ability to go from one failure to another with no loss
of enthusiasm.
Winston Churchill

Michael Carter

Don't be pushed by your problems; be led by your dreams.
Ralph Waldo Emerson

Change is inevitable; growth is an option.
At the center of your being, you have the answer;
you know who you are and what you want.
Lao-tzu

Man makes his own shipwreck.

The most beautiful days of my life have been those I have shared with you.

Dreams are never shattered, just rearranged,

Nothing matters more than more years together.

There is always room in your heart for more love.

A Nurse's Prayer
Lord, help me bring comfort where there is pain,
Courage where there is fear,
Hope where is despair,
Acceptance when the end is near, and
A gentle touch with tenderness, patience, and love.
VA Haley Veteran Hospital, Tampa, Florida

We must learn from yesterday's decisions to make the right choices today.

A human should not be judged only by the things they have done, but also by those things they did not do and what they left behind. Sometimes, our mistakes can change our lives and lead us in the right direction.

Music is the song of the heart.
"A midwife's song of freedom" by Patricia Hartman

Children grow in their own mysterious ways, not ours.

Maybe the mission of our life is to gain a better understanding and reason for our soul and spirit and who or what established our purpose.

◆▸◦◂◆

Maybe a form of God exists in each of us in our own unique and personal way.

◆▸◦◂◆

When life throws you a curve ball, hit it out of the park.

◆▸◦◂◆

Each of us needs to find our own identity and meaning of God.

◆▸◦◂◆

Each of us must find our own way to deal with our Goliaths.

◆▸◦◂◆

I'd rather be an hour early than a minute late.

◆▸◦◂◆

Maybe the world is round, so we can't see the end of the road.

◆▸◦◂◆

Contributors

Jennifer John for her artwork
Maya Angelou
Jan Batiste
Buddha
Edward Bulwer-Lytton
Susan Cain
Camus
Michael Carter
Rosalyn Carter
Cervantes
Charlie Chaplin
Chinese Proverb
Winston Churchill
Confucius
1st Corinthians 13: 4-8
Cyrus
Thomas Dewar
Emily Dickinson
Walt Disney
Bob Dylan
Albert Einstein
Ralph Waldo Emerson
Epictetus
Benjamin Franklin
Sigmund Freud
Robert Frost
Gandhi

German Proverb
Johann Wolfgang von Goethe
Stephen Grellet
Alexander Hamilton
Patricia Hartman
Arianna Huffington
Victor Hugo
Indian Proverbs
Michael Jordon
Joseph Joubert
Bryan Kalie
Santosh Kalwar
Bryon Katie
Larry King
Lao-tzu
H.L. Mencken
Napoleon
Shane Parrish
Thomas Payne
Fritz Perls
Michael Phelps
Colin Powell
Norwegian Proverbs
Eleanor Roosevelt
Theodore Roosevelt
Rod Sadleir
Judge Ester Salas
Susan Polis Schultz
Dr. Seuss
G.B. Shaw

Stendahl
Robert Louis Stevenson
Shunryu Suzuki
Alfred Tennyson
Henry David Thoreau
Turkish Proverbs
Veterans Administration Haley Hospital Tampa, Florida
Swami Vivekanada
Oscar Wilde
Zip Ziglar

About the Author

Michael Carter was born in Eugene, Oregon in 1940. His early years were spent in Oregon, California and Utah. After graduating from Franklin High School in Los Angeles in 1958, he attended Pasadena City College for one year where he was elected class president. In 1960 he joined the U.S. Army and was stationed at Ft. Liberty (Bragg) in NC where he completed jump school in the 82 nd Airborne and was honorably discharged in 1963 as a squad leader (E-5). He then trained as a computer programmer and went to work for United Airlines in Denver, CO. Being a single parent and looking for answers, Carter sold everything, packed up the kids, bought a sailboat and took a year off sailing in the Bahamas and Caribbean. Carter then settled in Pennekamp State Park and commuted to Miami to work at Eastern Airlines on the reservation system and obtained his U.S. Coast Guard Captain's License. After Eastern went out of business, Carter worked as a captain on a variety of boats including tug and barges, a research vessel, a paddle wheeler, a ferry boat and evening cruise boats. Carter and his wife also delivered boats for people and businesses. Carter then wrote user manuals for the marine industry and received his Master's in Technical Communication from the University of Central Florida. Carter later received an MBA in Management from Webber University in Florida. In the summer of 2002, Carter and his wife hiked approximately 750 miles of the Appalachian Trail. Carter settled in Lake Wales, Florida and from 2008-2012 was elected city commissioner and then mayor. Carter is currently retired and enjoys his time traveling and writing.